PRESENTED TO:

_____

FROM:

_____

DATE:

_____

OUR TRIP ACROSS AMERICA

BRUCE & STAN

Stories We Heard About

Joy

ON OUR TRIP ACROSS AMERICA

Bruce Bickel & Stan Jantz

Project editor—Terri Gibbs

Designed by Uttley/Douponce DesignWorks
Sisters, Oregon

ISBN: 08499-5736-2

Printed and bound in China

CONTENTS

Behind Every Life
is a Story.

W

e're two ordinary guys, but we had an extraordinary adventure. We spent the summer driving across the country. Now, that event isn't extraordinary in itself. In fact, many people have performed the feat. But most folks drive across country in an attempt to complete the task as quickly as possible. The memories of those trips are long hours on the inter-state, fast food wrappers scattered on the car floor, and no personal contact with anyone except the cashiers at the old-fashioned gas stations (the ones that have pumps and don't accept credit cards) and the occasional tollbooth operator. (People who are in a real hurry, or particularly antisocial, save time and avoid contact with even the tollbooth operator by keeping lots of coins in the car and using the "exact change" lane.)

Our trip was different. It extended over three and one-half months, so speed was obviously not an issue. We drove over 10,000 miles (which proves we didn't take the short route). But the *duration* and *distance* are not what made our trip extraordinary. The most intriguing aspect of our trip was the *people* we met and the *stories* they shared with us about their lives.

The purpose of our trip was to interview people. We were doing the research for a book (*Bruce & Stan Search for the Meaning of Life*), so we spoke with everyone, everywhere (even tollbooth operators and gas station cashiers). We had meaningful conversations with over 1,000 people. (That figure *doesn't* include the people we passed on the street or sat next to on the subway or stood next to in the elevator, with whom we exchanged limited pleasantries. Actually, we didn't even exchange pleasantries with the people in the elevators. We didn't want to break the unwritten rule of elevator etiquette, which prohibits talking or making eye contact.)

We expected to learn a lot about the meaning of life by talking to people (and we did). We learned so much, it could fill a book (and it has). But the unexpected pleasure was hearing the personal stories of the people we met. We heard fascinating stories about people. Some of the stories involved tragic events; some were encouraging. All of them were life changing—for the people who actually lived the stories and for us as we heard them.

Our lives will not be the same because of the people we met and the stories we heard. If for no other reason, we have a greater appreciation for people because we learned this very important lesson: *Behind every life is a story!*

What makes these stories so amazing is that they involve regular people. We didn't talk to any celebrities. Just plain folk. People like us . . . and you. (This assumes that you aren't chauffeured around in a limo and that you don't live in a mansion. If you're like us, you're more concerned about paying the mortgage than avoiding the paparazzi. In fact, we are only interested in "paparazzi" if it's a new flavor of Ben & Jerry's ice cream.)

In this book we have included several favorite stories we heard while "on the road." They all have a common theme of joy. Notice that we didn't say "happiness." Happiness is nice, but it can vanish quickly at the first sign of adversity or unpleasantness. Joy, on other hand, goes deep. It provides a sense of fulfillment that withstands and endures the difficulties of life.

Joy intensifies your happiness when things are going well, and it transcends discouragement and defeatism when times are tough. But you don't have to take our word for it. You can sense the substance of joy from the lives of the people who are profiled in the following stories. They come from completely different circumstances, and not one of them knows any of the others, but there is a resemblance among them all: a joy about life that is the essence of who they are.

We hope you'll be inspired by these stories. We were. Maybe they'll motivate you to reflect on your personal stories and the lessons you can learn from your own life. Perhaps they'll make you more interested in the life stories of your friends and your neighbors. Maybe they'll encourage you to be more interested in the people you don't know as well. Remember: *Behind every life is a story!*

Bruce & Stan

OUR TRIP ACROSS AMERICA
BRUCE & STAN

BEACON
Drive-In

Pepsi-Cola

TRY
SPARTANBURG'S
LARGEST
BANANA SPL

The Joy of People

We drove more than 10,000 miles on our cross-country trip, so we saw a lot of our nation's landscape. Unfortunately, much of that scenery is fast-food franchises. We tired of those pretty quickly. Don't get us wrong. We like burgers and fries (we aren't un-American), but after a while all those franchises looked the same and their culinary cuisine began to taste alike. We did our best to alternate between McDonalds, Burger King, Jack-in-the-Box, Wendy's, Carl Jr.'s, and Hardee's, but before long the names were the only distinguishing feature.

By the time our route led us into South Carolina, we had assumed that there was no other way to serve a burger than in this prepackaged, predictable, fast-food franchise

15

Everybody likes a person with a good sense of humor.

---

fashion. Then we drove into Spartanburg. Boy, had we assumed wrong.

They've got a burger place in Spartanburg that is like no other (at least none that we found, and we looked conscientiously). It's called "The Beacon." We aren't quite sure why. It's got a big sign on the corner in the shape of a lighthouse, but with Spartanburg being 250 miles inland, the risk of a ship being that far off course is rather remote. Webster (the word guy, not the little kid on the TV show from the 1980's) defines a *beacon* as something that sends out a warning. With that definition, The Beacon is aptly named. One look at the burgers is fair warning that you might have a coronary attack if you eat one. (We aren't kidding. There was an ambulance in the parking lot when we arrived.)

The Beacon is not a fast-food restaurant. Remember, this is South Carolina we're talking about. It's in the heart of the South—and nothing is fast in the South. You also have to remember that food isn't just for eating in the South. Every meal is an experience. And that's exactly what The Beacon is all about. It's a cultural event—the place were people come to watch and to been seen.

On any given day, you'll find politicians, plumbers, physicians, and postal workers sitting side by side. (And that's just the occupations starting with the letter "P.") Whether the diners are in a professional career or in the trades, whether they are adults or children, they all have one thing in common: the grease dripping down their forearms as they lift a chiliburger to their lips.

If you think
you can't give when you
have little,
then you won't give when
you have much.

The vocabulary of the English language is too limited to adequately describe the ambiance of The Beacon, but we'll try. The outside is decorated with numerous flags that flap in the breeze (much like your heart valves will be flapping to pump that cholesterol-laden burger fat through your veins.) When you enter, you stand at the end of a long, single-file line. When you reach the counter, you announce your order to J. C. Stroble. (You better be ready with your order. If you hesitate, you have to move to the back of the line.)

J. C. shouts out the order at a volume level normally used by people stranded on a deserted island yelling at a plane flying overhead. (From what we could tell, there's no one behind the counter specifically assigned to hear J. C.'s instructions.) You then proceed along the forty-foot long counter. You pass the cooking area where there are large vats of erupting chili each the size of a small spa.

A sense of humor is a sign of sanity.

GOD IS IN THE SMALL STUFF
FOR YOUR FAMILY

Alongside the vats are the burger grills. Although they look like they haven't been cleaned since they were purchased from Attila the Hun, we suspect that is one of the secrets to Beacon burger flavor.

Next down the line you walk by the frying vats. Wire baskets, approximately the size of a Volkswagen beetle, are filled with potatoes (of the french fry and hushpuppy varieties) and submerged into cauldrons of bubbling oil. At the end of the line you're handed a plate with the food you ordered. If it's your first time at The Beacon, you're sure you've got someone else's order, because you didn't order a meal large enough to climb. Then you're told, "No, that's just a single chili burger. That's what y'all ordered."

We won't say there's a lot of grease back in the kitchen, because we wouldn't want to get sued for libel (although truth is a defense). We'll just point out that The Beacon is the only restaurant we know where the cooking crew wears waders (you know, those rubberized trousers with built-in boots that fishermen wear). But that grease is important. It lubricates your throat to make it easier for the paramedics to insert the tracheotomy tube as they try to revive you from your coronary thrombosis.

There are two things that you have to understand about The Beacon.

First, the food is good. Really good. Sinfully good. (This statement presupposes that you aren't a vegetarian and that your favorite flavor is "deep fried.")

Secondly, the whole experience is fun. The people who

eat at The Beacon have a good time because the people who work at The Beacon make it that way.

Any astute businessperson knows that you need a great employee to be on the front lines dealing with the public. We're sure that's why The Beacon has J. C. Stroble standing at the front of the counter to take (and yell) your order. If you are a first-time diner at The Beacon, J. C. will joke and cajole that order out of you. If you come often (does that make you a "frequent fryer"?) he'll greet you like an old friend—because to J. C. you are.

Attitude is a funny thing. Your perspective on life is completely determined by your attitude, yet you get to choose the attitude you want. For example, if you have tough circumstances in your life:

- you can choose to be morose and wallow in self-pity; or
- you can be enthusiastic about the positive things in your life and ignore the negative ones.

Laughter removes all barriers.
When people are laughing together,
there is no young and old,
no boss or subordinate.

If you need a personification of a positive attitude, then we suggest you plan a little trip to Spartanburg, South Carolina. Stop in at The Beacon and watch J. C. Stroble in action for a while. You can stand to the side of the line and stare at him for hours. It won't bother him. He won't even know you're there. J. C. is blind.

At the risk of holding up the line (and being sent back to the end), we asked J. C. why he was so joyful all the time. "It's all about customer service," he said. "We love to wait on you. When we see y'all, we give you good service

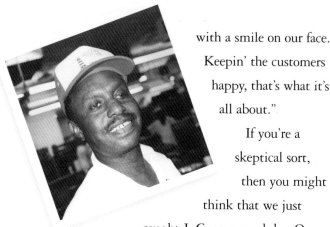

J. C. shouts the
burger orders at
The Beacon.

with a smile on our face.
Keepin' the customers
happy, that's what it's
all about."

If you're a
skeptical sort,
then you might
think that we just
caught J. C. on a good day. Or
maybe you think he was upbeat
and positive just because things
had been going well for him that
year. Well, he's been standing at
the counter greeting customers and shouting orders for a
lot longer than one year. "I've only been here forty-four
years," he told us. "But I'm trying to make forty more."

By even the most conservative estimates, J. C. Stroble

has shouted the food orders for literally millions of customers at The Beacon over the last four and one-half decades. Yet he's never seen a single one of those customers. It doesn't matter. He knows they're smiling. It's his job to make sure they are. And he does his job well—extremely well!

OUR TRIP ACROSS AMERICA

BRUCE & STAN

The Joy of Art

New York is the greatest city in the world. Everything about New York evokes energy and excitement. If you live there, you're probably aware of the impact your city has on the rest of us. In fact, you're not only aware, you take it for granted. You know that New York is the cultural architect for the world. Whether we're talking about fashion or food, business or Broadway, architecture or art—it all starts right there in the concrete canyons of Manhattan.

We scheduled only three days in New York (we know, a foolish plan), so if we were to find the meaning and the soul of the city, we had to choose a cultural category thoughtfully rather than digging into every individual cultural nook and cranny. We did this by eliminating those aspects of culture where we had a weakness.

Now, by observing the way we skillfully blend khaki and plaid in all social situations, you might think that fashion is our forte. It isn't. And while each of us enjoys a finely cooked meal just as much as the next guy, you're more likely to find us eating cheesecake at Stage Deli than *fois gras* at Sardi's.

As for business, well, we don't want to give away our secrets, but let's just say that retirement is still a few decades away. And while we enjoy a good Broadway show, but we'd just as soon see a revival of *Brigadoon* than some critically acclaimed play. We love good architecture, but the depth of our knowledge is revealed in a statement one of us made as we wandered the streets of New York: "Gee, I wonder if Jimmy Hoffa really is buried in the cement beneath Giants' Stadium."

As we saw it, we were down to one remaining cultural

Occasionally in life there are those moments of unutterable fulfillment which cannot be completely explained by those symbols called words. Their meaning can only be articulated by the inaudible language of the heart.

—MARTIN LUTHER KING

---

category, and that was art. But this posed a problem. Neither of us has studied art, we don't own any art (unless "Dogs Playing Cards" on velvet is considered art), and we doubt very much if we could appreciate much of the art the art critics appreciate. But we were into our second day in New York, and we'd eaten all the cheesecake we could stand. It was time to get down to business.

Fortunately, one of our contacts, a highly respected "culture vulture," gave us some advice. "You guys need to meet Makoto Fujimura," he told us. "He's one of the brightest and most thoughtful artists in New York today. He approaches his art through a Christ-centered worldview, but he doesn't work within the Christian enclave. Mako is a worldwide Christian with a worldwide reputation."

"So why would he want to meet with us?" we wondered.

"You're going to have to sneak up on him," our culture friend advised. "Here's his address, but don't use my name. I don't want my reputation sullied by you two in any way."

Still smarting from our contact's last remarks, we hailed a cab in midtown and instructed the driver to take us to Makoto Fujimura's studio on Greenwich Street in lower Manhattan. "I told you not to wear that shirt," Stan said. "That shows no taste whatsoever."

Beauty is
all about us, but how
many people are
blind to it!

—PABLO CASALS

"Hey, don't criticize my shirt," Bruce replied. "That cheesecake stain on your pants didn't help us one bit."

Thirty minutes and twenty dollars later, the cabbie dropped us off. Or more accurately, he slowed down the cab enough for us to roll out the back seat and onto the pavement. Before we could orient ourselves, the driver disappeared in a squeal of tires and a cloud of asphalt. We were expecting to be in the heart of New York's thriving art community (there are more than 400 galleries in Manhattan), but instead we were in the middle of a warehouse district, the kind you see in movies where they wheel sides of beef around on giant hooks.

We stood there in the middle of the street wondering if our culture contact had given us the right address, or perhaps didn't want us to return . . . ever. Fortunately, we had a phone number, and we dialed it. Mako answered and we did our best to sound legitimate. We were here to talk to

him about his art, and
we were referred by
his good friend the
culture vulture. We
asked him if we were in the
right place. Mako said we were on the right
street, but we were looking on the wrong side (the side
with the meat hooks). His studio was on the other side
(the side with the art studios).

   We made our way to Mako's studio, a very cool space in
a converted warehouse. Remember that this brilliant artist
didn't know us, but he invited us to meet with him. Also
keep in mind that Mako had just returned from Hong
Kong, where he had been installing a public art exhibition

True joy
is that earnest wish we
have of heaven, it is
a treasure of the soul.

—JOHN DONNE

sponsored by the Chinese government. He hadn't slept in more than thirty-six hours, yet here he was talking to us. We were impressed.

Our impressions were just beginning. As we sat down with this gracious artist, we quickly realized that we were in the presence of greatness. He didn't tell us that he was great. Mako is soft-spoken and thoughtful (a remarkable contrast to us). What spoke of the enormity of his talent were the incredible paintings in his studio and his unique approach to art. Within the first few minutes, we began to sense a passion and a certain joy emanating from this man and his work—a passion for his art and a joy for the One who gives his life meaning.

Makoto Fujimura was born in Boston. After completing an undergraduate degree at Bucknell University, he moved to Japan to study the technique of Nihonga (which is literally translated "Japanese style paintings") at the Tokyo

National University of Fine Arts and Music. He received his M.F.A. in 1984 and his doctorate in 1992. While in Japan, two things of major consequence happened to Mako. His knowledge of Japanese art and his skill in interpreting ancient art forms won him critical praise around the world. And he met the One who would change his life and his approach to art forever.

"When I transferred my allegiance from Art to Christ in 1987, causing my art to be Art," Mako said, "a shift occurred in my vision. Whereas before, I had an intellectual doubt of seeing reality as it is, let alone depicting it,

Mako explains the meaning of his art.

now my new-found faith gave me the foundation to see reality and to trust it. Colors and forms I saw were indeed what others could see, and the objective world did connect to the subjective."

We asked Mako to expand this idea further, and he gave us a brief art history lesson. Mako explained that artists lost faith in art at the end of the 1980s, so the 90s became the decade of doubt. Artists found they lacked the certainty of an absolute foundation. Basically, they didn't trust reality, so they attempted to reach transcendence in order to capture "the fear and power of the age." And that's where we are now, in the twenty-first century, with "no cohesive meaning out there."

Even though he uses materials and techniques developed over a thousand years of Japanese painting, Mako employs the visual vocabulary of twenty-first century art. You would call Mako's paintings abstract or semi-abstract, but you wouldn't see the despair so prevalent in modern art. If you were to see the bright colors—extracted from precious and semi-precious mineral pigments—and the rich textures—drawn from biblical themes—you would detect hope and joy.

"I see abstraction as a potential language to speak to today's world about the hope of things to come. My works exegete both classical Japanese works and contemporary American paintings. I interpret them in a way, hopefully, that will increase the viewer's passion for seeing the physical reality and heavenly reality."

Mako paints in what he calls "sacramental language," which by its very nature "must address reality and confront what we see, but must transcend it to grasp what we can't see yet."

The New York art critics have seen in his art what Mako describes in words. Robert Kushner wrote: "The idea of forging a new kind of art, about hope, healing, redemption, refuge, while maintaining visual sophistication and intellectual integrity is a growing movement, one which finds Fujimura's work at the vanguard."

In fact, Mako founded the International Arts Movement (IAM) in 1990 to "unite artists with Christ-centered spiritual direction." His eyes sparkle when he talks about reaching other artists with his sacramental language. In one particular image entitled "River Grace (red)," Mako painted a thin gold line from the top to the bottom of the piece. "The golden thread of God's grace can be so thin, you and I are likely to miss it in the hustle and bustle of everyday life," Mako explained. "But once we do notice God's grace in our lives, also like the golden line, it dominates the whole, making us aware of its significance and dominance in our lives."

Perhaps it's the recognition of God's grace in his life

that gives Mako his greatest joy. "I want to play a role, hopefully, to redeem the language of art, so that we can all, Christians and non-Christians alike, use the language to communicate," Mako said. "We need to; the greatest celebration and cosmic wedding awaits us. We need to be ready, and invite others to join us, to rejoice, dance and sing . . . and paint."

Suddenly all of the great food and high fashion that so many people associate with New York paled by comparison to the lofty images of hope and joy we had just seen. In the light of God's grace and the eternity that awaits us, the bright lights of Broadway and the ticker tapes of Wall Street seemed insignificant. Here in this nondescript studio were reality and truth, and they did indeed cause us to rejoice, dance, and sing. The good news is that it didn't cause us to paint. We'll leave that to Makoto Fujimura and his immeasurable talent, vision, and joy.

Bruce & Stan
try to get a
little culture
by visiting
the Metropolitian
Museum of Art
in New York City.

THE WOOLWORTH
BUILDING IN
NEW YORK.

OUR TRIP ACROSS AMERICA · BRUCE & STAN

Joy Reunited

We weren't looking for it. We didn't even know it existed. But in our travels we came across the most emotional strip of land in the U.S.A. (Actually, the *ground* isn't emotional, but it evokes emotion from the people who walk over it.) Can you guess what it is?

No, it's not the Vietnam Veterans Memorial wall in Washington, D. C. (although everyone visits it with a somber and respectful mood).

And it's not the land at the base of the Statue of Liberty where you stand as you gaze up at her. (Lady Liberty is best viewed from a distance anyway. If you stand too close and look up, you just have an unattractive view of her nostrils.)

Based on our wholly unscientific observation techniques,

we think the most emotional piece of ground is that strip of about 100 feet in front of the door at each airport terminal gate. This is the path across which all passengers walk as they disembark from the plane. The space where they are either: (a) greeted jubilantly by family and friends with hugs and kisses; or (b) overcome with a sense of loneliness as they proceed by themselves to baggage claim.

Whenever we're killing time in an airport (which is usually longer than the duration of our flight), we enjoy watching reunions at the airport gates. It's a fascinating study in the joy of family and friendship. You can spot the passengers who are expecting an awaiting entourage; they immediately start gazing across the gathered crowd to find a familiar face. And the assemblage of greeters all start craning their necks to look down the corridor that connects with the plane to get the first glimpse of the loved-one whose arrival has been long awaited. You can hear shouts

If there's one place
we all long to go,
it's home.

GOD IS IN THE SMALL STUFF
FOR YOUR FAMILY

of "Here she comes!" or "There he is!" Then there are shrieks of joy and screams of gladness as the arriving passenger goes through the ritualistic ceremony of hugging, kissing, and occasional high-fiving each member of the reception party.

If you ever want a glimpse of true joy, go hang out at the airport. Look for a group of greeters who are carrying signs, noisemakers, and flowers. You'll see the celebration of a lifetime. And don't be surprised if you hear a comment like, "I can't believe you've been gone for a whole week." You see, the sense of joy isn't determined by how long you've been apart. It's all about getting back together.

Learn to recognize
the non-verbal signals of
your family members.

GOD IS IN THE SMALL STUFF
FOR YOUR FAMILY

OUR TRIP ACROSS AMERICA · BRUCE & STAN

We're two guys (you'll have to take our word for it), and we know what kind of job every guy fantasizes about. No, it isn't being a professional athlete. Young boys dream about that, but they don't know any better. It takes a few years of maturity to recognize that professional athletes run a substantial risk of being injured or stalked. Walking with a limp and a sore back from the age of thirty to the grave doesn't appeal to us. Neither does traveling incognito with sunglasses, a ball cap, and a beard. (Bruce can't even grow a beard, and Stan can't endure the indignity of "hat hair.")

Professional athletics is not the career we dream about. (And we suspect the same is true for every other rational-thinking male over the age of . . . well, let's leave it at rational-thinking males, although that may be an oxymoron.) We've determined that the career of choice would have to be that of a high-ranking corporate executive for an international sporting goods company. Think of it: all the perks of a professional athlete, without the risk of bodily harm from competitors or rabid fans.

- International travel in private, luxury jets.
- A fat corporate expense account.
- An unlimited supply of sweat pants. (We could throw away the ones we've been wearing since we were sophomores in college.)
- A pick-up game of basketball with Michael Jordan.
- A round of golf with Tiger Woods.
- Tickets to the Super Bowl, the World Series, Wimbledon and the NBA Finals. And not just any tickets, but "Oooh, I must be in the front row" tickets.

Every guy wants a sports-related career.

We have to stop. It's enough to make a guy's pulse race and his face go flush.

You might think that a dream job like that would be all a guy needs to have a complete life. We sure did. That was until we heard about Matt Hennessee.

We don't know what *careers* women dream about, but we have been told about the kind of *guys* that they dream about: guys who are tall, dark, and handsome. Our reliable source of information on this subject is our wives. When we heard their assessment, we pointed out that neither of

When it's all said and done,
the greatest legacy you can leave is
a life centered on God.

us is tall, dark, or handsome. We didn't even get one out of three. (Our wives said that they were painfully aware of that fact.) In a feeble and transparent attempt to salve our dignity, our wives explained that they made the "tall, dark, and handsome" determination after eliminating us from consideration due to some sort of conflict of interest technicality. If it hadn't been for that glitch, we're sure that they would have identified us as every woman's ideal man.

You might be wondering what the "tall, dark, and handsome" criteria have to do with Matt Hennessee. Well, when a woman conjures up a mental picture of "tall, dark and handsome," Matt is the guy that pops into her mind. He has got all the components:

- He's tall: He stands in at 6'2".
- He's dark: Matt is an African American.
- He's handsome: He is one great looking guy (and we are comfortable enough with our own masculinity that we aren't afraid to admit it).

It should be enough that one guy gets either the good looks or the dream job. One or the other, but not both. So, if Matt Hennessee is every woman's Adonis, then fairness dictates that he should be stuck with some repulsive job. (A scuba diver for Root-M-Out Sewer Cleaning would do just fine.) But oh, no! Through some fluke of nature, or some misalignment of the planets, or perhaps due to the hole in the ozone layer, Matt Hennessee became the Director of Global Operations for Nike Inc.

Just hearing about Matt's circumstances made us jealous. We figured it was our responsibility to resent him (not just for ourselves, but on behalf of the rest of the male population who hadn't heard about him.) But the people who knew him all spoke so highly of him that we wanted to meet him. So, we routed our cross-country trip through Portland for that very purpose. (We decided that if he told us to "Just Do It," we would tell him to "Just Shove It.")

You only need to spend a little time with Matt before you agree that he *is* a great guy! That's what happened to us. He has a genuine interest in people. He gives you his undivided attention, and you feel like he considers you to be one of his best friends. (It's hard to dislike a guy like

Matt Hennessee striking a pose.

that; we tried our best, but even we couldn't do it.)

Matt isn't interested in talking about himself. (Maybe that's why people sense that he's sincerely interested in them.) But we wanted to know what his life was like. We wanted to hear about his adventures as the head honcho for the global operations of the Nike sporting goods empire. We wanted to hear some "up close and personal" stories about our favorite pro athletes, and we wanted to live vicariously through his stories about the famous sporting events he attended.

The more you remember
what God has done in your
life in the past, the more
you will see Him at work in
your life in the present.

But Matt didn't want to talk about all of that. He was excited about something else.

That "something else" is the St. Paul Missionary Baptist Church. For more than ten years, Matt has served there as an associate pastor. As you can imagine, Matt is loved by the people in his church; it's a response to Matt's servant attitude. You see, that's what gives Matt joy in life— serving the people in his church. So, as pastor, interspersed between his corporate duties, Matt visits members of his church in their homes, he visits them in the hospital, he prays for those who needed comforting, and he handles the burying and the marrying, too. And perhaps most important of all, he preaches God's Word on Sunday mornings.

When Matt's job at Nike requires him to be out of town on a Sunday, there are others in the church who pinch-hit for him. But if at all possible, his corporate schedule is designed to accommodate his responsibilities at

God can speak to you through the Bible, but you can't hear Him if you keep the cover closed.

---

the church. He doesn't mind the complicated, logistical gyrations to make it happen because being with his church family is what he wants to do most of all. When something brings you joy, it isn't an inconvenience to fit the details of your life around it.

(Since our visit with him, Matt has resigned his job at Nike. He is now the President and C.E.O. of Quiktrak in Lake Oswego, Oregon. But one thing hasn't changed: you can still find him behind the pulpit of the St. Paul Missionary Baptist Church on Sunday mornings.)

Most guys can't find enough time and energy after work to take out the garbage or mow the lawn. Matt Hennesse always manages to do those things (although it's frequently the garbage or lawn of someone in his church). Apparently, there's plenty of time in life to do the things you find most rewarding. It might mean you have to miss a pick-up basketball game with Michael Jordan, but it's all about what gives you the most joy.

Joy's Perspective

Without meaning to cast aspersions, it's our experience that a human stomach can only tolerate roadside restaurants for a limited time. So, whenever possible on our cross-country trip, we tried to finagle an invitation to someone's house for some good home cooking. Surprisingly, we were successful on quite a few occasions. Sometimes it was for Sunday dinner. Other times it was a backyard barbecue. But every time, it was a "family gathering."

We're two family guys ourselves, so we know about the joy that comes with having the entire family gathered together. This is not how television programs usually portray families. Television usually goes to the dysfunctional side of the familial spectrum for laughs or drama. The families we know actually enjoy getting together and aren't plotting swindles or murders against each other. And we don't know of a single family that is filled with the full compliment of the Simpson characters (although we do know a few Homers).

As we attended these family gatherings, we noticed that the grandparents were often sitting to the side with smiles on their faces. They weren't in a catatonic state. (We know because we checked.) They were just savoring the moment of seeing their family—their kids, and in-laws and grandchildren—all enjoying each other's company.

Savoring the moment!

Family traditions
communicate values much
more effectively than
a lecture.

The parents were too busy to enjoy this perspective. They were busy corralling the kids or attending to the logistics of the dinner. (The dads were frequently preoccupied with dosing the flames that were erupting from barbecues and trying to salvage charred remains of steaks.) But the grandparents were sitting back, appreciating the scene.

Every time we witnessed such a scene, we were reminded of this verse:

I have no greater joy than to hear that my children are walking in truth (3 John 4, NIV).

Unfortunately, we could never think about it for long. The pensive moment was usually interrupted by screams for someone to drag the garden hose over to the barbecue.

Instead of finances,

make your greatest gift to

your children a rich heritage of

personal qualities such as integrity,

joy, and spiritual sensitivity

to God.

OUR TRIP ACROSS AMERICA

BRUCE & STAN

The Joy of Service

Many of the cities we drove through didn't make much of a first impression on us. Let's face it. A lot of cities look the same at first glance. They've got buildings, roads, businesses, and residential areas. So, for many of them, they give a first impression that is nondescript. That isn't true, however, for Washington, D. C.

Even a casual drive through the nation's capital can take your breath away. You'll see the majesty of the Lincoln Memorial. History and current events seem to intersect as you see the White House and recall the number of presidents who have lived there in your lifetime. You may be overwhelmed by a sense of democracy when you pass the Capitol Building. And there's another feeling you might get: a gnawing in your gut when you realize that you helped pay for everything you see.

After you spend a few days in Washington, you get a sensation that is found nowhere else in the country. It's called "Potomac Fever," and it's what draws so many young professionals to Washington. Now, we know as much about government as most Americans (we had a civics class in the seventh grade, we studied U. S. history and government in high school, and we watch The West Wing television series). But we didn't really know much about "Potomac Fever." We figured it must be either:

- a retro disco club in Georgetown;
- a phrase used to describe a politician's decline in the popularity polls (as in "he's coming down with a bad case of Potomac fever"); or
- one of those CNN talk shows where people with opposing political viewpoints yell at each other.

It didn't take long in Washington to realize that this city has a magnetism that draws people to it. We think it's the aura of power that pervades the city. It's like an aphrodisiac that attracts the young, educated, professional types. They want to be in the middle of the power plays that determine our nation's course. They are infected with . . . Potomac Fever.

In many respects, politics is like a game of sports, and there are a lot of people who like to play it. We've basically got two "teams" in this country, with players and fans on each side. Like all sports, people can get really intense

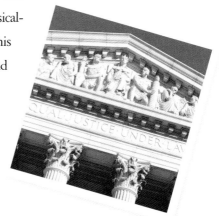

One of the great halls of power.

What you earn affects
the quality of your living;
what you give affects the
quality of your life.

when they play. (There may be fewer obvious physical injuries in politics, but perhaps more ulcers. There are "stress-related fractures" in politics, too, but this usually refers to a politician's marriage.) Politics can give you the thrill of victory, but the next vote may bring the agony of defeat. (Just ask Al Gore.)

We met two individuals in Washington who have managed to transcend the emotional roller coaster of politics by finding joy outside of their jobs. Don't get the wrong impression. They have important jobs, and they're good at what they do (very good or they wouldn't still have them). But for these two women, their greater sense of satisfaction comes outside the halls of Congress, and inside prison yards and the homes of the poor.

Like so many of the young professionals in Washington, Townsend Lange McNitt got her first taste of Washington while she was still in college. As a junior at Gordon College she interned with Senator Dan Coats (R-IN) who was then a representative and the ranking Republican of the Select Committee on Children, Youth, and Families. What she did after graduation wasn't so typical: she spent eight months volunteering at an eighty-bed orphanage in Zimbabwe, Africa.

After returning from Africa, Townsend attended law school at the University of Notre Dame. Her law studies included one year at the Concannon Program of International Law at the Notre Dame London Law Centre in England. With her law degree, she returned to Washington

Encouragement costs nothing, and yet it pays tremendous dividends.

Bruce with Townsend Lange McNitt, a high-ranking Senate staffer devoted to service.

and was appointed as special advocate by the D. C. Superior Court to represent abused and neglected children.

Townsend currently serves as chief counsel and chief policy advisor to Senator Judd Gregg of New Hampshire. She also manages Senator Gregg's twenty-five-person Washington office staff. Despite the demands of her job, Townsend spends much of her free time advocating the rights of foster children. And she also volunteers with Georgetown University Law School's Family Literacy Program, serving inmates in two correctional facilities in the D. C. area. All of this extracurricular volunteer service is prompted by the lessons she learned from the orphans, nuns, and local people in Africa who had so much joy in their lives. As Townsend tells it:

"The people I worked with had nothing compared to American standards. Though they wanted more, they weren't consumed with desire for more. I learned much from them about being content in whatever my circumstances."

In a town where people seem preoccupied with what they can take, Townsend Lange McNitt finds personal joy in *giving* to others.

Denzel E. McGuire came to Washington after graduating from the University of Virginia. She's the Senior Staff Member of the U. S. Senate Subcommittee on Children and Families. This woman is passionate about helping others.

Denzel McGuire finds her greater fulfillment working with people outside Washington's beltway.

(And that's not just our opinion. Her friends call her "On Fire McGuire.")

With Denzel, passion is more than just a personality trait that diverts boredom. She told us that she considers it a necessary part of the job: "Passion is the number one attribute required to effectively implement public policy. It keeps you on your feet, and it helps you keep your perspective."

We wondered how Denzel managed to keep her

*Encouragement is anatomical—
it sometimes requires a pat on the back.*

passion at such a high level on a constant basis. "Doesn't it ever wear thin?" we asked. "You can't achieve that passion through your job alone," she answered. "To keep that passion going, it's imperative to volunteer, to have some interaction with the lives of the people that your policies impact."

For Denzel, that interaction happens several times a week as she visits one of the poorest neighborhoods in the D. C. area during her off-hours and assists with a child literacy program. She explained that her volunteer work allows her to personalize the legislation she is drafting.

"I think it's imperative that you have real world exposure when you're considering how a particular policy will affect children. When you work inside the beltway, there's a danger that you'll have 'beltway blinders' and end up just drafting paragraphs, or sentences, or words as part of some legislation. Unless you volunteer, you don't have a real connection with the lives you're impacting. So very often as I'm looking at some legislation, I try to think how this is going to affect a particular child with whom I have a relationship through my volunteer work. I try to keep the faces of those individual children in my mind."

It seems to us that many people in Washington are interested in only the *public* part of "public service." They want the limelight. In contrast, Townsend Lange McNitt and Denzel E. McGuire emphasize the *service* part of "public service." They are servants in the truest sense, and they get a lot of joy out of it.

OUR TRIP ACROSS AMERICA

BRUCE & STAN

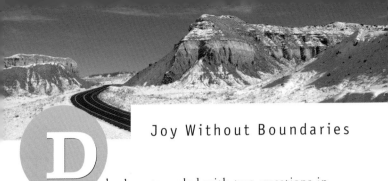

Joy Without Boundaries

Deby has struggled with two questions in her life: *Where is that special place?* And *How can we show the world?*

It wasn't easy, and it didn't come quickly. But the place has been found, and now she knows *how*.

Deby was born into an athletic family. Her parents were professional skaters for the Ice Capades. Since her dad was an acrobatic ice skater, Deby was tossed and flipped in the air more often than most infants. She must have enjoyed it, because as a young girl she pursued gymnastics. She was following in her parents' footsteps (but without the blade

> *The first duty of love is to listen.*
>
> — PAUL TILLICH

on her shoes). She was also good at it. Very good.

Deby's younger sister, Kathy, was even more excited about gymnastics. Except Kathy didn't have Deby's athletic ability. Some people said that Kathy didn't have any athletic ability at all. You see, Kathy has Down's Syndrome.

As children, Deby and Kathy enjoyed practicing their gymnastic routines together in the family yard. Deby would serve as Kathy's coach, and they both felt a sense of accomplishment and joy when Kathy would master a new routine. But when they went to the gym, it was a different story: Deby was given an enthusiastic welcome while Kathy was turned away. Deby still remembers the heartache she felt when people would say, "Kathy can't practice with us.

There must be a special place for people like her." That's when Deby began asking herself the question:

Where is that special place?

That's all Deby wanted to know: Where is the place where Kathy can be coached to have the same fun in athletic activities that are so readily available to other children? At that time, no such place existed.

Deby didn't stop asking that question as she grew older. Even when she was in college and having tremendous personal success in gymnastics at the national level, she was concerned about Kathy's desire to train, compete, and perform.

Just when her gymnastics career appeared to be heading for greatness, tragedy struck. Deby had been accepted as a member of the U. S. Olympic trial team, but she suffered a career ending injury. Most other athletes might harbor a lifetime of bitterness over this circumstance, but Deby no longer sees it as a tragedy at all. It's what God allowed to happen because He had greater plans in store for her life.

About this same time, Deby was dating Steve Hergenrader. Steve was also an athlete. He had been playing professional baseball in the farm system for the New York Yankees. Like Deby, he suffered an injury that ended his playing career. Their sports background gave them something in common, but common experiences don't always mean that a man and a woman will be compatible. That happens when they share similar values. Deby knew that Steve had the type of character she was looking for in a husband when she saw how he interacted with Kathy. He always gave Kathy the attention and respect she deserved. He was also interested in helping her with her sports activities. That part of Steve's character is what made him so attractive to Deby. (She says the fact that he is handsome was just an added bonus.)

Few things
in life are as easy
to give, and have as
much impact,
as encouragement.

The backyard of Steve and Deby Hergenrader's house was a little unusual. It had a trampoline. That's not so unusual. But it also had a pommel horse, a balance beam, and "gym mats" which Steve had made himself out of foam rubber and carpets and old bed mattresses. All of this paraphernalia was used by Deby as she continued to train Kathy in gymnastic skills. As other parents of disabled children heard what Deby was doing with her sister, they asked to include their children in program. They didn't have to ask twice.

BTB—a sports & arts program.

Many of these other children had able-bodied brothers and sisters, and Deby invited them to be part of the group.

Before long, Deby had gymnastics classes in her yard every afternoon. She had more student athletes than she could handle. But you would have the wrong impression if you thought Deby's backyard gymnastics academy was a "handicapped program." You'd be way off. Deby was teaching gymnastics—plain and simple. Some of her students were physically disabled, others weren't. It was no big deal either way. They all learned together. They competed with and against each other. They all laughed and encouraged each other to achieve their own personal best (at whatever level that might be). It was an arrangement that pleased everyone.

For the first time in their lives, Kathy and the other disabled children had a program that didn't exclude them. They were experiencing the joy of accomplishment. They weren't being pitied or ignored because of their physical limitations. Maybe they were learning differently or more slowly, but that just added to everyone's thrill at their personal achievement.

The able-bodied children were also being trained. For them, however, the training was not just in gymnastics ability. They were learning to appreciate their disabled teammates in a whole new way. Some of these children had no previous contact with anyone having a serious disability. Now they were cheering them on.

The parents were learning, too. For most of them, the concept of integrating the able-bodied and the disabled in sports was revolutionary. They acknowledged society was long overdue for a revolution of this sort. People were beginning to catch the vision for the benefits of sports activities that include both able-bodied and disabled children.

But Steve and Deby were learning the most of all:

Serving the able-bodied and disabled.

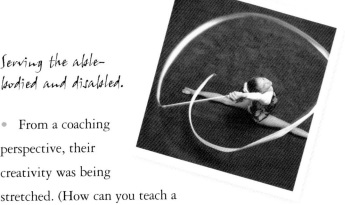

- From a coaching perspective, their creativity was being stretched. (How can you teach a backward flip to someone who has no legs? With the child's unlimited determination, the only holdup is the coach figuring out how it can be done.)
- They were also learning that their backyard was not big enough.

It was officially incorporated under the name of "Break the Barriers," but is affectionately known around town as "BTB." It's a sports/arts program for the able-bodied and disabled. Steve and Deby were the founders and executive directors, but BTB received community-wide support from the start.

After a few transitional sites, BTB was able to occupy a vacant supermarket building. With donations, and fundraisers and provisions that couldn't be anything other than miraculous, BTB took shape as a full-fledged sports and art center. Classes were offered in:

Gymnastics

Dance

Martial Arts

Weight Training

Drawing

Sign Language

Baton Twirling

There are bleachers just inside the entrance to the building. This is where the parents sit and watch during classes and during the performances and competitions.

Most of the time those bleachers are surrounded by the students' backpacks, bikes, skateboards, wheelchairs, and crutches. It's all normal stuff at BTB.

BTB was a dream come true for Deby. But more than that, it answered the "Where is that special place?" question that had been plaguing her. *Break the Barriers* is the special place where kids like Kathy can experience the thrill of sports.

Almost as soon as the "where" question was answered, another one popped into Deby's mind: *How can we show the world?* The people who were involved with BTB—students, parents, and instructors—knew how their lives had been changed by BTB's inclusive approach for the able-bodied and disabled. But other people needed to come to this realization. Deby was asking herself how she could show the world what Kathy and the others had to offer. It wasn't something that could be easily publicized. Skywriting or

The BTB was a dream come true for Deby.

pamphlets hung on door-
knobs couldn't convey the
heart and soul of what
these kids were all about. It
was something that had to be seen to
be appreciated.

Deby chose some of the BTB athletes to be in a
performing group. They called it the "Barrier Breakers."
By now in this story, you ought to know that Deby didn't
pick the best athletes to be in the group. That's not the
standard by which people are evaluated at BTB. She

picked the ones with the biggest hearts (which included some kids with malfunctioning hearts). This group worked up a few routines to music, using their tumbling and gymnastic skills. These routines had to be especially choreographed to work in the wheelchair athletes and others with physical limitations. It was Deby's plan that the Barrier Breakers would perform at a program for the parents in the BTB gym.

Deby's plans were disrupted by a single phone call. One of the BTB coaches was also the cheerleading coach at the University. She had learned that the entertainment for the half-time program at the University's next basketball game had just cancelled. Would BTB have any interest in putting on the half-time show? You already know the answer.

There were a few frantic days as Deby attended to the final details. The Barrier Breakers scheduled some extra practices, and someone was assigned the responsibility of purchasing some sort of uniforms. (Blue bodysuit leotards were chosen.) Deby recruited Steve into the Barrier Breakers because they needed a spotter, and he agreed. (That was before he realized what uniforms had been selected. From Yankee pinstripes to BTB blue bodysuits. Only love would make a guy do it.)

Most basketball half-time shows are just ignored. Their sole purpose is make noise and occupy the floor while people go to the bathroom and get some refreshments. But a funny thing happened at half time during the University's next basketball game. No one left his or her seat. At first it was sheer curiosity that kept people there. The invasion of Smurf-like kids running and wheeling onto the gym floor. It was obvious that some were able-bodied. It was even more obvious that others weren't. People wondered about this strange affiliation.

After the first few minutes, people no longer stayed

Bruce does the "man on the street" interviews in Chicago while Stan eats pizza nearby.

THE OLD WATER TOWER IN CHICAGO.

ACROSS AMERICA

BRUCE & STAN

out of curiosity. They stayed out of amazement. They were stunned by the gymnastics; they were impressed by the tenacity of these athletes; and they were moved by the obvious camaraderie shared by those on the floor. At the end of the performance, 10,000 people were on their feet applauding; and 20,000 eyes were welling up with tears.

Deby's second question was suddenly answered. That night marked the beginning of what has been a constant tour of performances by the Barrier Breakers. They perform at high school assemblies, community service organizations, major sporting events and educational conferences. Each performance tells a story and teaches the lesson. The story is about BTB. The lesson is what Deby learned as a young child practicing gymnastics with Kathy in their parents' yard: That the participation of able-bodied and disabled together in sports changes everybody's life for the better.

The great thing
about caring for others
is that you will always
be a person
others feel comfortable with.

The Joy of God's Creation

Three thousand years ago King David stood on a rooftop and gazed up at the sky in wonder. Later he penned these immortal words:

The heavens tell of the glory of God.

The skies display his marvelous craftsmanship.

Day after day they continue to speak;

night after night they make him known.

They speak without a sound or a word;

their voice is silent in the skies;

yet their message has gone out to all the earth,

and their words to all the world.

The sun lives in the heavens

where God placed it.

Joy is the

serious business

of heaven.

C. S. LEWIS

It bursts forth like a radiant bridegroom
after his wedding.
It rejoices like a great athlete
eager to run the race.
The sun rises at one end of the heavens
and follows its course to the other end.
Nothing can hide from its heat.
Psalm 19:1–6

There is something about the heavens that fills us with wonder and joy. Like David, you can't look up at the night sky without being filled with awe. You can't consider the magnitude of the universe without thinking about God.

There's a simple reason for this, and there's a technical reason as well. The easy explanation for why "the heavens tell the glory of God" is precisely because that's the way God designed it. The apostle Paul explained: "From the time the world was created, people have seen the earth and sky and all that God made. They can clearly see his invisible qualities—his eternal power and divine nature. So they have no excuse whatsoever for not knowing God" (Romans 1:20). You could say that God put His designer label on His creation, and it says, "Made by God."

The more technical reason for thinking about God when you consider the heavens has to do with science. When David gazed at the stars, he could see 5,000 at the most (that's the maximum number of stars anyone can see with the naked eye). Four hundred years ago, when Galileo first used the telescope to view the stars, he could see hundreds of thousands of them. Modern telescopes disclose as many as 125 billion galaxies, which may contain over 200 billion stars *each!*

Using these high-powered telescopes and space satellites, today's astronomers have been able to peer into

Bruce gazes into the heavenlies... sort of.

the deepest corners of the universe. They have literally looked at the beginning, when the universe came into being. And what have they concluded? Robert Jastrow, one of the world's top astronomers and a self-confessed agnostic, put it this way: "Every star, every planet and every living creature in the Universe owes its physical origins to events that were set into motion in the moment of the cosmic explosion. In a purely physical sense, it was the moment of creation."

Here's how the Bible puts it: "In the beginning God created the heavens and the earth."

All of these thoughts were swirling in our heads on a beautiful, sun-splashed day in California. We were walking the campus of the University of California at Berkeley, which has one of the most esteemed science faculties in the world. We had heard about one science professor in particular, Dr. George Smoot, whose work in the field of astrophysics had led to "the discovery of the century."

Using a satellite called the Cosmic Background Explorer (COBE), Dr. Smoot and a team of astrophysicists were successful in measuring the radiation "ripples" that

Dr. George Smoot, who led the team that first measured the beginning of the universe.

came from that first cosmic explosion. "What we have found is evidence for the birth of the universe," Dr. Smoot declared in 1992, when the COBE findings were announced. "If you're religious, it's like looking at God."

As we ascended the hills of Berkeley to meet with Dr. Smoot in his office in the Lawrence-Berkeley Lab, it suddenly dawned on us. We were going to be interviewing a man who has literally seen the beginning of the universe!

Honestly, we were expecting to meet someone who was absent-minded and aloof, speaking in a language we could barely understand. We were way off. From the moment George Smoot waved us into his office, we found this world-class scientist to be down-to-earth, engaging, and enthusiastic. We asked him about COBE, and he pointed to something in the corner of his office. "That's a piece of the prototype for COBE right there." We were mesmerized. In our offices we have paper clips and notebook computers.

This guy had stuff that reached back to the beginning of time!

Rather than using scientific jargon, Dr. Smoot conversed in a way we could easily understand (and that's quite an accomplishment). Mostly it was his almost child-like sense of wonder that impressed us. Dr. Smoot had every reason to reduce his knowledge to a set of scientific principles. (Isn't that what scientists do?) Instead, he talked about the possibilities that lay ahead. His demeanor was joyful as he talked about the things science will discover in the years ahead.

As we left the Lawrence-Berkeley Lab that day, we

reflected on God's creation, especially the stars. The Bible mentions stars a number of times, so they must be important. God created them (Genesis 1:16), and remarkably, "He counts the stars and knows them by name" (Psalm 147:5). Perhaps most importantly of all, God used a single star to announce the birth of His Son, Jesus.

When the ancient astronomers of the Middle East saw that Star of Bethlehem, the Bible says "they were filled with joy" (Matthew 2:10). Their reaction is a reminder to us that everything in God's creation—especially the stars—should fill us with joy and cause us to thank the God who made it all.

OUR TRIP ACROSS AMERICA

BRUCE & STAN

The Joy of Overcoming

Joy can take many forms. The most direct route to joy is to experience something immediate and totally unexpected that you had nothing to do with. But there's a deeper joy that comes after what C. S. Lewis called "the inconsolable longing." King Solomon, the wisest man who ever lived, put it this way:

Hope deferred makes the heart sick, but when dreams come true, there is life and joy" (Proverbs 13:12).

Think back to when you were a kid, waiting for Christmas morning. A large part of the joy you felt when the big morning finally arrived was because you had waited so long (almost making yourself sick in the process). If you're married, you can well remember the joy of your wedding day made even better because you waited.

Then there are those times of difficulty, times you think will never come to an end. You dwell in darkness for an extended period, and then suddenly—sometimes without warning—the light breaks through and the joy you feel is beyond description. We've all been through this cycle, and because we know that joy waits for us on the other side, we need not fear the darkness. That's why James wrote to the Christians in the first century who were experiencing persecution:

Dear brothers and sisters, whenever trouble comes your way, let it be an opportunity for joy (James 1:1).

While we were in Boston, we heard about a story of hope deferred and dreams fulfilled. It's a story you may have heard about as well, because you undoubtedly have heard of the person involved. But you've never heard the story quite like this.

"In the 1992 Olympics, I felt God's pleasure."

Paul Wylie is a legend in Boston, and a legend in Olympic skating. While he was a sophomore at Harvard, Paul competed in the 1988 Winter Olympic Games in Calgary. He was one of three Americans vying for a medal, and one of the team's biggest hopes for gold. But it was not to be. He fell in the final round, failing to win a medal of any kind. Paul Wylie didn't quit, however. After his disastrous spill, he got up and continued his program with style and class, endearing himself to the crowd in the arena and millions watching on television.

"I've learned so much about God and my relationship with Him from such experiences," Paul later wrote. "I've seen, in other areas of my life, that God wants to lift me when I fall, and He provides me with a way to leave my mistakes behind, redeeming them and using them for His purposes."

Not only did God pick Paul up that night, but He did something even more remarkable four years later at the 1992 Games in Albertville, France. Notice we said *four years.*

Paul's hope for an Olympic medal had been deferred, and the journey back to joy took four years. During this time Paul's success at the world-class level was moderate at best. He never finished higher than ninth in any world championship. Paul Wylie, once considered one of America's most talented ice skaters, strongly considered retirement, especially after he graduated from Harvard.

Friends and family encouraged Paul to give it one more

Don't be
dejected and sad,
for the joy of the Lord
is your strength!

—NEHEMIAH 8:10

"When I run, I feel God's pleasure."

—ERIC LIDDELL

shot. "Don't limit the Lord," a good friend advised him. "All you need is the faith of a mustard seed." Paul decided to compete in Albertville, training harder than ever to overcome what he called his "nemesis"—the triple axel. He turned the corner when he changed his thinking about the very technical move.

"From my quiet times, I began to feel that God wanted me to turn my attitude about triple axels upside down," Wylie wrote. "Instead of seeing the jump as nerve-wrackingly strenuous and difficult, 'The Jump I Dreaded' needed to become, well, *fun*. The shift in attitude from dread to fun, even joy, came as I tried to imagine God's perspective on my life."

"In the 1992 Olympics, I felt God's pleasure," wrote Wylie. The skater soared through the preliminaries, the short program, and the long program. He hit his triple axels with confidence, and the French crowd loved it. When the competition was over, Paul Wylie stood on the victory stand with a silver medal. For him, it was the realization of a dream and the expression of incredible joy.

"When I look back on that moment, it always amazes me to think that the omnipotent God, the creator of galaxies light years away, will give us His strength and grace to help us in all of our struggles—in our relationships, in our careers, and even in things that seem insignificant to others. He sees our hearts, and He wants us to acknowledge our needs and rely on His help. All we need to do is ask—and rise as He lifts us up."

The Joy of Expression

We saw the Blue Man Group before the Blue Man Group was cool. Okay, so maybe they've been selling out their off-Broadway show in New York since 1991, but hardly anyone outside of their cult-like following in Boston (where the Blue Man Group started) and New York knew they existed. Now the Blue Man Group is pitching Intel processors on television, and they have their own major show on the Las Vegas strip.

Admittedly, we didn't know who the Blue Man Group was either, but when a student we met in Boston heard we were going to New York, he pleaded with us to see the show. "They'll even let you in for free if you agree to be an usher, but you have to get there like an hour early." Ah, the joys of youth!

When we got to New York, we decided to take in the Blue Man Group show as two regular paying, non-ushering customers. The Astor Place Theatre, the permanent home for the Blue Man Group, is about as far off-Broadway as you can get and still be in New York. There weren't any tourist-types hanging around this part of Manhattan, especially when we went to Max's Deli (New York's oldest) for a pastrami sandwich and some cheesecake before the show. We're not going to say the place is old, but the top layer of linoleum at Max's looks like it was installed right after World War II—and that's on the counters. The floor has so many layers of linoleum you have to be careful not to turn your ankle in one of the crevices.

But you don't go to Max's for the atmosphere. The food is to die for (we don't mean that in a literal sense). If you go to Max's Deli, don't worry about making a decision from the rather complicated (for a non-New Yorker)

The Brooklyn Bridge and the New York City skyline at night.

wall menu. The burly and surly deli guys behind the counter will tell you what to order.

"I'll have mayonnaise on my ham sandwich."

"No, you don't want mayonnaise, and you definitely don't want ham. You'll have a pastrami on rye with mustard. Will there be anything else?"

"No, that looks fine, unless you have another suggestion."

"Of course, you'll have one of these enormous New York style pickles that's been fermenting in a pre-war barrel we keep in the back."

"Of course."

After our experience at Max's, we made our way to the Astor Place Theatre, where a few people were already lined up. Thirty minutes before showtime, they let us into the "lobby," which was a subterranean room lined with hundreds and hundreds of plastic tubes—all kinds of tubes, from vacuum cleaner hoses to PVC pipe to the kind of tubes you hook to your laundry dryer at home. (We were about to see the Blue Man Group in a production called "Tubes," so the décor was appropriate.) Inside the theatre, there were even more tubes, along with dozens and dozens of rolls of toilet paper hanging from the ceiling on brackets (more about that later). The theatre was long and sloping, with a small balcony. We estimated that it held no more than 300 people, and by the time the curtain went up, every seat was filled.

We were sitting there ready for the show to begin when a voice called out from what seemed like thin air.

Grand Central
Station in
New York City.

THE
CHRYSLER
BUILDING

Lunch in Central Park.

When large numbers
of people share their joy in
common, the happiness of each
is greater because each adds
fuel to the other's flame.

—ST. AUGUSTINE

"Hey, is anybody there?" We looked around, but nobody was looking at us. The voice called out again. Then we realized it was coming from one of the tubes under the chairs. We picked up and answered back, yelling directly into the tube. "Who's this?"

"I'm back stage. Where are you all from?" We answered, and by now several people sitting around us were involved in the conversation. Then we got the bright idea to ask this Blue Man Group backstage guy the question we ask everyone. "What's the meaning of life?"

Without hesitation, he shot back through the tube, "Expression. That's the meaning of life. We humans are the only cognitive beings capable of expressing ourselves, and so we need to do that. Now enjoy the show!"

Enjoy was a very accurate description of our experience for the next ninety minutes. It was totally enjoyable. Unlike so many other entertainment extravaganzas that leave you flat, here was a live theatre experience that flat-out delivered *joy*.

After a very clever pre-show, which involved a simple scrolling electronic message board, the three Blue Man Group performers came on stage to the sound of pulsing music. Actually, *pulsing* isn't completely accurate. *Pounding* is more like it, because the searing guitar rhythms and riffs are augmented by a bass drum twice the size of the kind used in marching bands. When one of the Blue Man Group performers lays into that drum with a mallet that looks like it came from the shinbone of a Mastodon, the sound waves rattle your chest.

Each Blue Man Group member looks the same: simple black shirt and pants and completely blue skin (at least their shaved heads and hands are painted blue). They never say a word, but their message comes across loud and clear: laugh, don't take yourself too seriously, be curious about

Blessed are the joymakers.

—NATHANIEL PARKER WILLIS

things, and don't let the stress and demands of our modern world overshadow the joy of life.

We weren't the only ones who got this message. At the end of the show, someone from the back of the theater started unraveling the rolls of toilet paper (remember, we're talking dozens upon dozens of giant rolls of unbreakable toilet paper). Everyone in the audience grabbed these streaming wads of paper and sent them forward, until you had several gigantic piles of (recyclable) heavy-duty toilet paper at the front of the auditorium. Meanwhile, the music was blaring, strobe lights were flashing, and people were laughing. This went on for at

People who know God personally should be the world's greatest enthusiasts, because we have the greatest reason to be excited about life.

least ten minutes until the rolls were empty. And that was the show.

When the house lights came up, we stood and looked around. Every single person was wearing a grin the size of Alice's Cheshire cat, and when we saw how joyful everyone else was, we smiled even more! For the first time that either one of us could remember, we were in a place completely filled with *joy.*

Had we just experienced an earthly slice of heaven? Were those Blue Man Group performers something like

Blue Angels, and the rest of us mere mortals tasting the innocent pleasures of unabashed joy? Maybe we're over-spiritualizing things here, but there was definitely a lesson for those of us who claim to have the joy of the Lord in our hearts. When we think about what the Lord has done for us, we ought to be wearing expressions of joy instead of looking like we just tasted one of those giant pickles from Max's Deli.

I will be filled with joy because of you. I will sing praises to your name, O Most High" (Psalm 9:2).

More Stories

We invite you to read some of the other stories
we heard in the course of our cross-country tour of America.
They have been collected in three additional books:

Stories We Heard About Love
Stories We Heard About Hope
Stories We Heard About Courage

And here are some other books we've written,
some of which are quoted in this one:

God Is in the Small Stuff
God Is in the Small Stuff For Your Family
onyourown.com
Bruce & Stan's Guide to God
Bruce & Stan Search for the Meaning of Life

We'd love to hear from you. You can reach us by email at
guide@bruceandstan.com or through our Web site:
www.bruceandstan.com.